THE HIGH-BALLER'S BALLAD

BY
MEGAN & ALAN WAIN

ILLUSTRATIONS BY
DANIELLE ADAMS

Raspberry Press

Written by Megan & Alan Wain
Illustrations by Danielle Adams

Published by Raspberry Press

Copyright © 2024 by Megan Wain & Danielle Adams

Cover design by Danielle Adams
Book design by Danielle Adams

Paperback ISBN: 978-1-0691325-0-5

Raspberry
Press

This book is dedicated to the TemChap planters whose grit and crazy humour made even the worst times a blast, and for all tree planters whose spirit lives on in the forest.

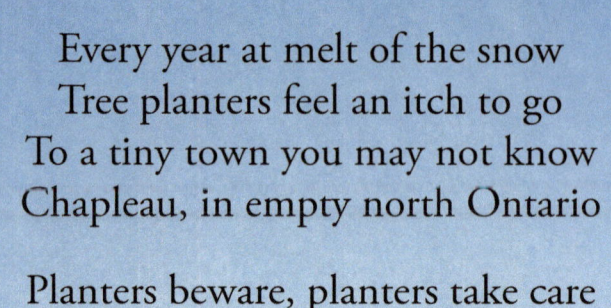

Every year at melt of the snow
Tree planters feel an itch to go
To a tiny town you may not know
Chapleau, in empty north Ontario

Planters beware, planters take care
For let me share, declare and swear
That something odd, something rare
Once happened in the forest there

Forgetting the dirt, the bugs and the rain
Forgetting the bears, the bees and terrain
Forgetting fatigue, the pain and the strain
The planters re-gathered to give 'er again

The usual suspects made up the crew
Vets from Torawna, the Peg and the Soo
And yes it's true, more than a few
Innocent rooks had been lured there too

There's no way I'll remember 'em all
But if memory serves, if I recall
That was the year of Andy the tall
Ben the high baller, and Mandy the small

Seen at the scene: the lean Kathleen
Calm, yet keen, a queen of serene
Quality clean if you glean what I mean
Not a has-been, still a planting machine

And…

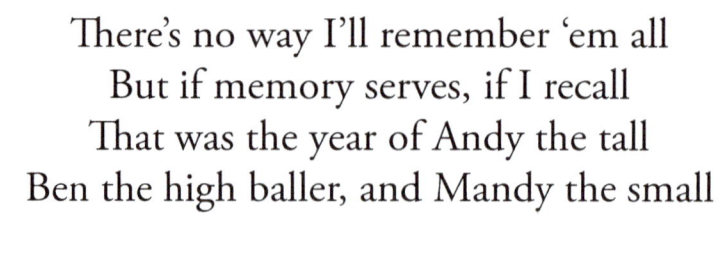

Ernie the Earnest and Artie the Artist
(Talented guy but a flatulent fartist)

That guy who was chronically happy and huggie
Smiley and silly young Dougie the Druggie

Buddy the Buddhist and Rudy the rudest
Semi-clad Clara, who was nearly a nudist

All-business Howie, just there for the cash
Partying Woot-woot!, so up for a bash

Bear-fearing, bee-fearing, snake-fearing Dwayne
Too long in the woods, and no longer sane

Musical Gabe and his bit with a git
Go-go, his dancer, and Willie the wit
Fit-throwing Patience, prone to a snit
And know-it-all Nolan, notorious twit

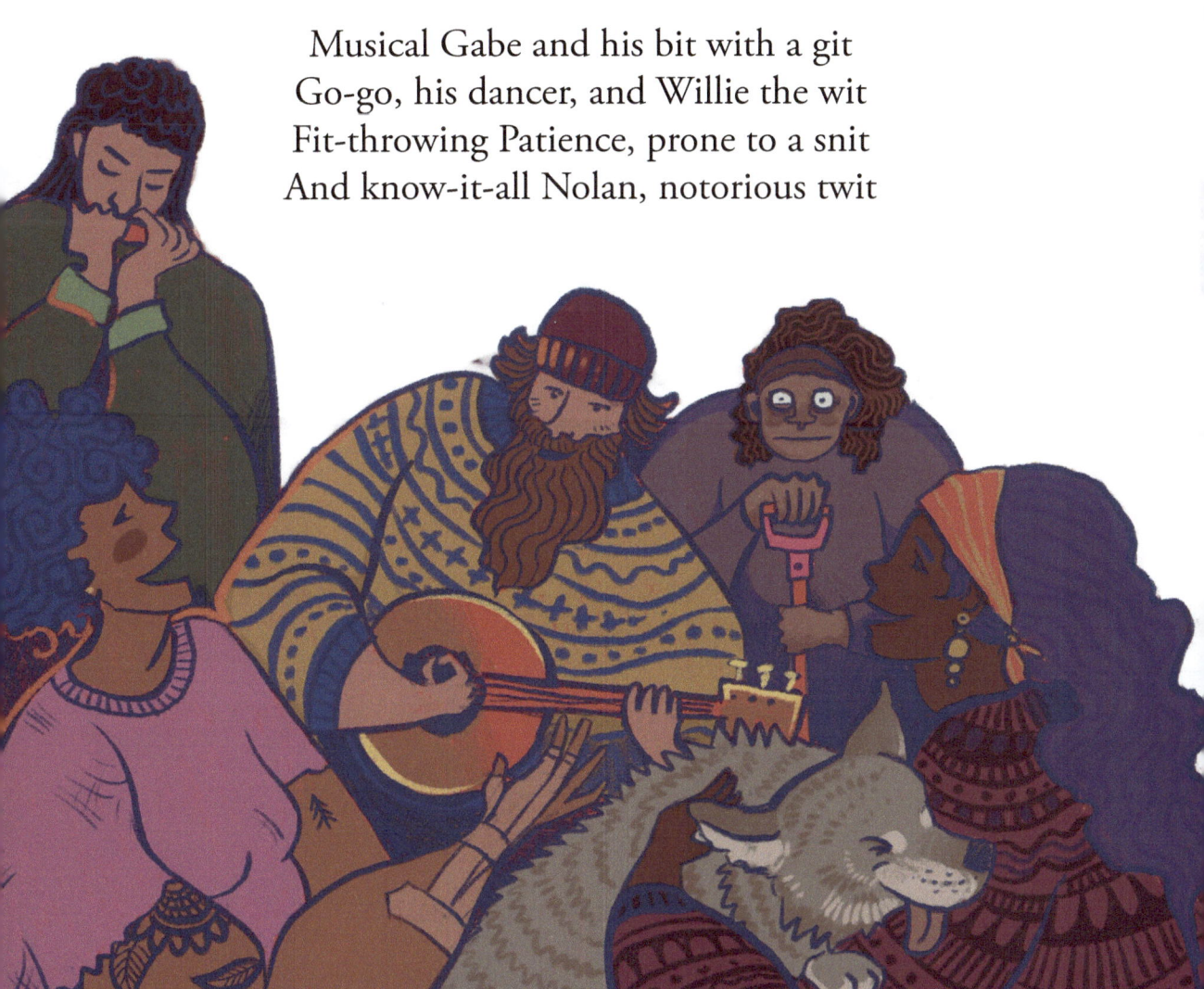

Each gal was a jewel
each guy was gem
But listen up hosers
it's not about them

It's mainly about him
and mainly about her
The things that they did
and the way that they were

I'm talking about Peggy, the fabulous she
And Morris who went by Magnificent Me
While Mo the magnificent most often ranted
Peg was quite simply, I'll say it, enchanted

Rumour had it and gave it to me
A forest a day planted Peggy Magee
With glee for her fee, she planted a tree
Tree after tree, then tree after tree

How she stayed spotless was talk of the block
As we all got filthy, her whites stayed like chalk
Her hair always looked like she'd shampooed each lock
While we stumbled in muck, she danced over rock!

On us, blood-sucking skeeters would hone
Making us swat them, cry out and moan
But when Peg said, "Please stop" in a very soft tone
The skeeters said, "Sorry" and left her alone

Dead trees called chichoes filled us with dread
A bonk from their branches could make a man dead
But chichoes loved Peg and protected her head
When she was below they fell elsewhere instead

It's part of the job to get injured and sneezy
Feverish, sweaty, pale, barfy and queasy
Blistered and sore, worn out and wheezy
Yet Peg stayed hale and made it look easy

Meanwhile two decades ago…

Northwest on a farm somewhere near Lake La Barge
To a soldier Sarge and his lovely Marge
A babe was born with an ego too large
Always believing himself in charge

Sweet diapered athlete
Not yet on his feet
Crawled to compete
In his blankey track meet

He bothered his kith, he bothered his kin
Burrowing deep under everyone's skin
Bragging: "Peerless am I, without a twin
My only sin is I always win."

It wasn't okay, acting that way
Causing dismay, till they sent him away

To us

This pest from the West came brimming with zest
On a quest, we guessed, our patience to test
Such a bad guest, not even in jest, without request
Claimed: "Planting's a contest and I am the best."

I wish I could tell you this chum was a bum
I wish we had sent him back where he came from
It makes me quite glum to admit that, in sum
He was rich, he was clever, and damn it! – handsome

Blue eyed and rock jawed and fit from his farm
Deep voiced he gun-showed a bump on each arm
Manly, calling everyone near him to witness his charm
Oh how we loathed him and wished him such harm!

An ire provoker, this unfunny joker
A cheater at poker, a Bogarting toker!
If you prefer Pepsi, well he was a Coker
You know the type? An annoyance evoker!

All through the summer, a rivalry grew
We all saw it building but what can you do?

The whole big mess if I had to guess
Stemmed more or less from an excess of stress

Our throng did its best to all get along
With a happy song and a lit peace bong
But we couldn't stop it from all going wrong
'Cause we planted and planted and planted too long

Oh, ay, what can I say?
What's under control sometimes slips away

T'was in the Bee Hell of August when as I recall
Dougie, much stung and unstrung, asked for us all:

If a rock needn't rock
And a wok needn't walk
If bark needn't bark
And a park needn't park
If the sea needn't see
And a pea needn't pee
Then tell me, oh tell me:
Why must a bee be????

We grew bush-whacked and sore-backed
Gob-smacked and jaw-slacked
Slash-hacked and untracked
So sacked and mood-blacked

I remember poor Dwayne, a million-tree man
Nervously chanting: "I think I can, I think I can,
I know I can… I hope I can."
Found he couldn't and off he ran

Our happiness level began to retard
For checker Trish McDecker was riding us hard
Judgmental Trish, that coldest of fish
The faults she would find, the disses she'd dish!

Says Trish:
"No plant must ever slant.
You see that slant upon your plant?
De-plant that plant.
Replant that plant.
And this time,
make your plant not slant!"

I've recalled that day again and again
The torrential showers, followed by rain

You know how some days just totally suck?
Well this was a day Peg ran out of luck
Slipped in a swamp, got stuck fast in muck
Cold, filthy, slimy and ewww! I mean yuck!

She couldn't plant trees, she could not earn a dime
It felt so unfair. It felt like a crime
To waste all that time, just pickling in slime
With her shouts unheard, she felt like a mime

Without any food she grew very hangry
As hungry and angry as anyone can be

Hour upon hour with nothing to do
But stick in the goo, feel blue and stew

Finally, at long last, came end of the day
The crew forgot her, packed up, drove away

When they finally came back, she was fit to be tied
When she entered the mess tent we gave a berth wide

All she wanted was food. All she needed was food
All the long day, she had been dreaming of food
Longing and craving and raving for food
Glorious, nutritious, delicious food!

But oh what's the matter? There arose such a clatter
When mad as a hatter, she rattled each platter
Saying, "Nothing is left. Just gravy splatter."

Then an aroma cut straight through her gloom
She perked up and exclaimed, "Va, va, va, voom!"
For the sweet smell of num-nums was strong in the room

She ran to them anticipating that glorious love at first bite
But she wasn't to taste them. No, not that night
For at the last minute an in-coming pest

Magnificent Morris, that pest from the West
Swooped in for one num-num, plus all the rest

Then he ate and he ate
And he ate and he ate
And he ate and he ate
And he ate
Until not a smidgeon of num-num
Remained on the plate

Obliviously treading upon her last nerve
He blissfully chewed up each last hors d'oeuvre
Saying, "Listen up lady, learn and observe
My rule is simple: first come, first serve."

Because he was what he was, he just had to add:
"I know that you crave them. I see that it's true."
But boo-hoo and poor you, I don't give a poo
I've eaten your yum-yums and not just a few
You'll just have to lump it. There's naught you can do."

It was like a volcano went off in her head
Smoke poured from her ears, her skin went all red
Such an eruption! The things that she said!
We blushed and we wondered if she were ill-bred

Then he reared on his hind legs (and this part is odd)
He bellowed and snorted and at the ground pawed
He sputtered and pointed yet only could nod
For as a debater he was rather flawed

Boss Nolan then burped out an idea so terribly bad
As bad as the worst one that boss ever had
To rile up the girl and to egg on the lad
And make even madder the already mad

A pox on you Nolan, notorious twit!
You found their fuses and made sure they got lit

He said:

"Grab up your shovels and strap your bags on
We'll settle this thing with a plant-off at dawn."

We hollered, we squealed because neither would yield
As they marched to that field on Canadian shield

They ran on sandwich power plus glare and glower
While planting future bower, hour after hour

How they kept it up, I do not know
They must have made their mojos flow

Though energy flagged, they would not let it show
It always looked go, go, go, in the foe versus foe

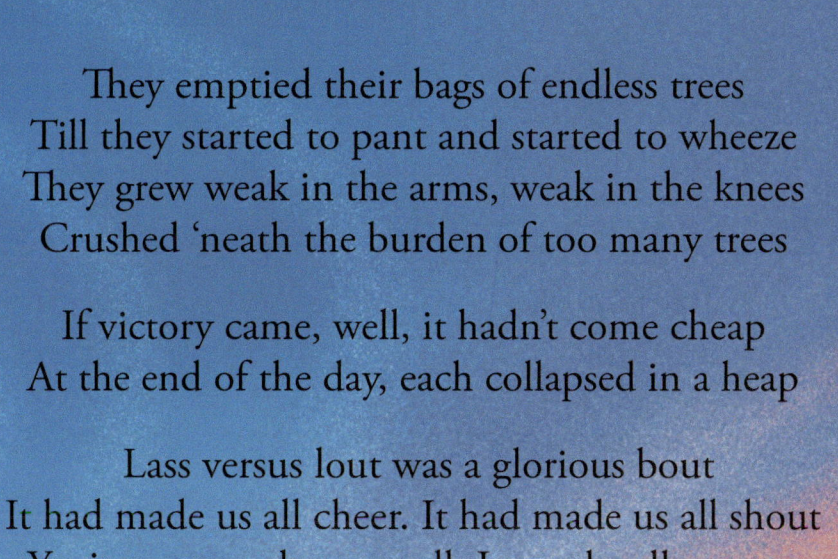

They emptied their bags of endless trees
Till they started to pant and started to wheeze
They grew weak in the arms, weak in the knees
Crushed 'neath the burden of too many trees

If victory came, well, it hadn't come cheap
At the end of the day, each collapsed in a heap

Lass versus lout was a glorious bout
It had made us all cheer. It had made us all shout
Yet it was too close to call. It was hardly a rout
They ended their day with the outcome in doubt

We consulted the owls, those fowls said to be wise
Whom won, do you think? What do you surmise?
But to our surprise, those fine feathered guys
Were wondering too, asking: Who? Who? Who?

In earnest our Ernest took up the count
As tension tensed up and started to mount

Finally, Ernest said Morris' tally was done
His exact total: "a ginormous sum…
plus twenty-one."

We let out a moan at the number so high
Oh drat! Oh fie! Peg could not beat that guy

The pressure immense got a tad too intense
So, Nail-biting Hortense withdrew to the tents

Then Ernie announced Peg's tally was done
Her total: a ginormous sum…
plus ninety-one!!!

How we cheered, how we danced
Knowing the gas bag's ego was lanced
Our joy felt enhanced.
So, that's when we pranced

I canna deny the flames that we fanned
We teased him too much. It got out of hand
Our bad behaviour should have been banned
We're lucky the lot of us didn't get canned

But Morris, he brooded and mused
Til from his brain, a Grinchy thought oozed

Says he, "Oh Sister Peg my planter-girl twin
How delighted I am by the mood you're all in
What a glorious ruckus and wonderful din!
And all 'cause Good Me let Little You win"

That jerk implied he hadn't tried
The guy, he lied! And I must confide
I was fit to be tied, prone to be snide
He was hard to abide. Yet Peg only sighed

Still, that barking pup just never let up
He wouldn't give up, wouldn't shut up

He asked her to see he was better than she
Kept calling himself "Magnificent Me"

Well, Patience could only take just so much of that
She picked up his gauntlet to renew the spat
She volunteered her good bud, our poor dear Peg
To take down the blow-hard just one more peg

So, they grabbed up their shovels
and strapped their bags on
To settle this thing
with a rematch at dawn

But wouldn't you know it, this time for a switch
The victory went to THAT SON OF A … gun

Then Nolan had one of his ideas bad
As bad as the worst that he ever had

Says he:

"Well it's clear to me, so I'll tell it to thee
The law of the land in the land of the tree,
Is when it's one-one, here's what should be,
I'm thinking tiebreaker: best two of three."

So they grabbed up their shovels
and strapped their bags on
To settle this thing
with a rematch at dawn

A pox on you Nolan! Notorious twit!
You re-found their fuses and now they're re-lit

But the next day they were still not done
'Cause best two of three meant our Peg had won
For the Pest from the West, that was no fun
So he made up a rule: no wins by just one!

I hate to report
It makes me so blue
Stubbornness doomed him
It doomed her too
They could never be done
They could never be through
Each could beat the other
but never by two

We watched with dismay as they lost their way
We begged them to stay but their plant-off a day
Carried them further and further and further away
Where did they end up? I really can't say

North of Superior?
East of Inferior?
In the Interior?
Oh my, it's dreary there

Well, the northern lights have seen queer sights
But the strangest one for me
Is when that ego large from Lake LeBarge
Made off with our Peg Magee

I wonder, are they planting still?
Her stubborn way, his iron will?

You've probably got doubts as I once had mine
Until I got that sign that shivered my spine
This soft quiet line from a whispering pine

Singing, "Grab up your shovels
and strap your bags on.
We'll settle this thing
with a plant-off at dawn."

Oh how I quaked! Oh how I shook!
When more confirmation of things in this book
Were overheard from a semi-coherent babbling brook

Singing, "Oh, Ay. What can I say?
What's under control sometimes slips away."

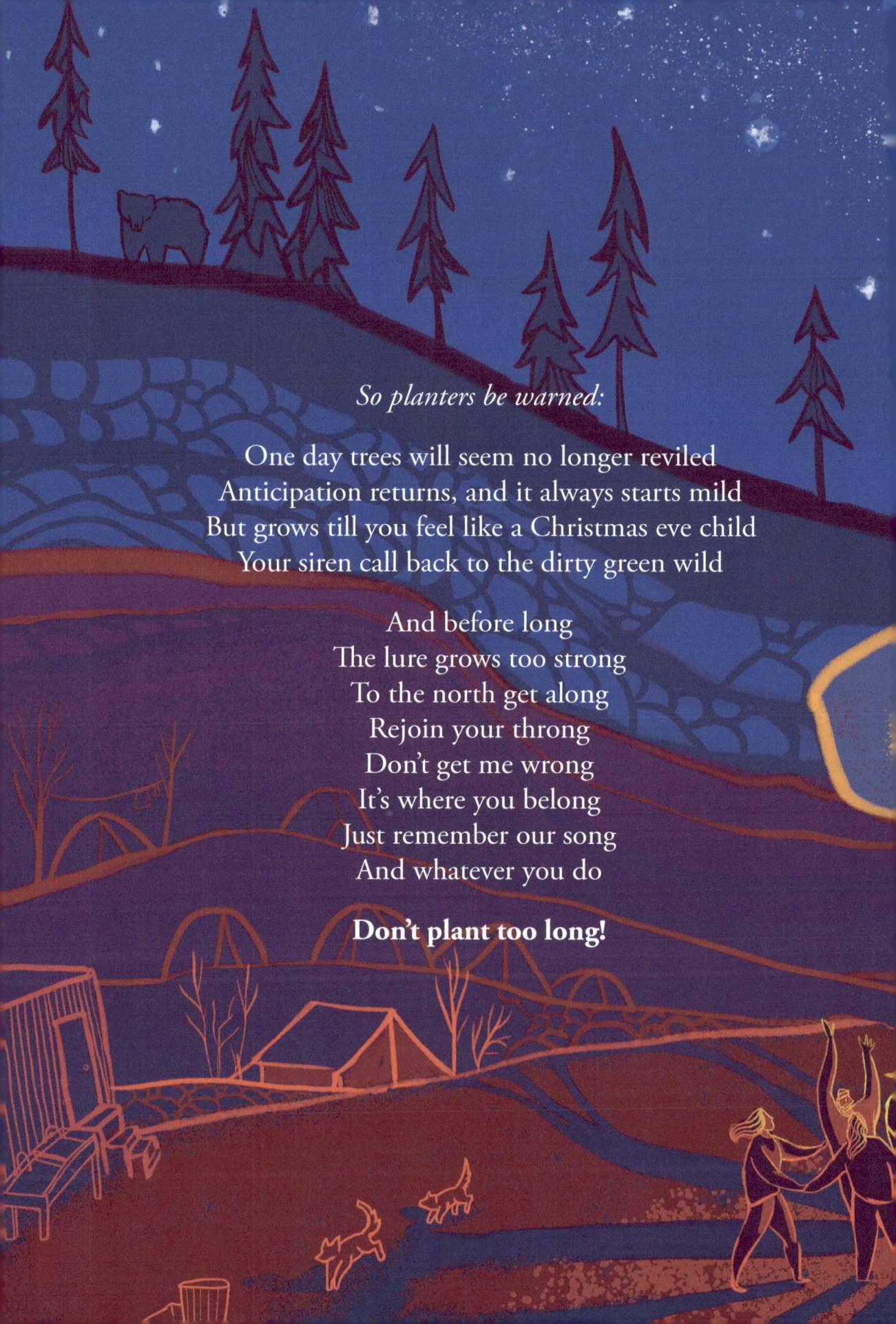

So planters be warned:

One day trees will seem no longer reviled
Anticipation returns, and it always starts mild
But grows till you feel like a Christmas eve child
Your siren call back to the dirty green wild

And before long
The lure grows too strong
To the north get along
Rejoin your throng
Don't get me wrong
It's where you belong
Just remember our song
And whatever you do

Don't plant too long!

ABOUT THE AUTHORS & ILLUSTRATOR

Megan Wain is a consulting arborist who planted more than one million trees over six seasons in Northern Ontario. She's no stranger to the extremes that can make even the sanest of planters go a bit bush crazy.

Alan Wain is the author of *White Death*, the harrowing tale of a group of researchers who get lost while looking for traces of the ill-fated Franklin expedition in Canada's far north.

Danielle Adams is an artist and illustrator from the Coast Mountains of BC. She paid for her fancy design and illustration degree by planting trees in Northern BC for four seasons. That time spent in the woods working with such colourful characters has had a huge influence on her artistic style and she secretly dreams of maybe going back for just one more season…

ABOUT RASPBERRY PRESS

No matter where you are in the book publishing process, from an idea on the back of a napkin to a finished manuscript, Raspberry Press can assist you to make your book a reality.

Cheryl Fountain is the founder and CEO of Raspberry Press. As a believer in following dreams, her goal is to make publishing a positive experience and to help authors get their books out into the world affordably.

Raspberry Press is an independent publishing consultation and service company that aims to help authors self-publish. Their goal is to make the publishing process as smooth as possible, and to encourage authors and artists to bring their messages and visions out into the world.

Raspberry Press offers personalized publishing consultation, self-publishing services, and publishing packages that will fit any publication no matter the size or genre. Authors retain full owner-ship and control when publishing with Raspberry Press.

To learn more, please visit *www.raspberrypress.ca* or email *info@raspberrypress.ca*

www.ingramcontent.com/pod-product-compliance
Lightning Source LLC
Chambersburg PA
CBHW042320250626

47164CB00016B/59